Houghton Mifflin Harcourt
Modern Chemistry

Engineering Design Guide

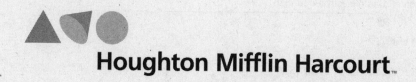

Houghton Mifflin Harcourt

Contents

Modern Chemistry Engineering Design Guide

Lesson 1: What Is Engineering?

Engineering and science are closely related, and in fact, engineers and scientists often work together to solve problems of interest to both. Despite their close connection, however, the two fields have distinct goals. *Engineering* applies scientific principles to design and build products and processes that are useful to humankind. *Science* is the system of knowledge humans have about the physical world and its phenomena, based on observation and experimentation. Put less formally, science is a way to study the natural world, whereas engineering is a way to achieve practical solutions.

Both science and engineering rely on evidence and follow a structured investigative process that may involve data, mathematics, models, and computational thinking. Both fields involve asking questions and solving problems. Scientific investigations generally ask questions to develop explanations for phenomena. Engineering studies ask questions to help define a specific problem and find a solution. Both science and engineering are interrelated with technology.

Technology

In its broadest sense, *technology* is the application of scientific knowledge for practical purposes. Technology is a process as well as the goods, services, and products that result from that process. Some of the earliest technology included the use of simple stone tools to do work and two-wheeled carts to move goods and humans. Today, many goods are mass-produced in vast factories utilizing complex machinery controlled by computerized systems; similar systems control the transport of those goods across the globe. Technology, then, can be said to include all human-designed and human-produced solutions and tools.

Modern technology touches virtually every aspect of the human environment, from agriculture and manufacturing to computer science and the aerospace industry. Viewed that way, technology can seem like something that involves only "big things." Yet technology touches every part of your life every day. Look around your classroom. Just about everything you see is the result of technology. The notebook on your desk, the pencil in

your hand, the shoes on your feet, the cell phone in your pocket, the water bottle and snack bar in your backpack—even the backpack itself—were all designed by engineers and produced using technology. Without technology, life would be very different indeed.

Types of Engineering

Engineering is a large and complex field composed of many branches and subspecialties that, in turn, serve many industries. Here are some examples of the types of engineers.

- Mechanical engineers design engines as well as all kinds of other machines: from cars and robotics to toys and roller coasters.

- Electrical engineers work in a wide range of fields, from power companies to defense contractors. They also design software and develop consumer electronics, such as smart phones and televisions.

- Closely related to electrical engineering is computer engineering, which helps develop computers, computer-based solutions for a range of industries, and of course, computer games.

- Chemical engineering serves a diverse array of industries, from large-scale production of industrial chemicals to pharmaceuticals. Chemical engineers also may work closely with environmental agencies to find solutions for recycling and similar problems.

- Civil engineers are critical to public works projects, such as building bridges, highways, and dams. Some civil engineers find ways to bring clean water to the public.

- Various engineering subfields in the life sciences involve solutions for producing food, pharmaceuticals, and biofuels, as well as protecting the environment.

The Connection Among Science, Technology, and Engineering

Science and engineering are closely interconnected with technology. The work of scientists brings knowledge that engineers draw on when designing solutions to solve a problem or meet a practical need. These solutions may then drive advances in technology that enable further scientific investigations. For example, the early achievements of scientists working with electricity led engineers to create power grids that brought electricity to homes, businesses, and public areas across the world.

The work of engineers, in turn, creates technologies such as microscopes, measuring instruments, and imaging software that scientists rely on to do work and conduct research. The development of the Hubble Space Telescope made it possible for astronomers to expand our knowledge of Earth's place in the universe and brought insight into the origins of stars and galaxies. The James Webb Space Telescope will extend this reach into the universe. Even development of a seemingly humble instrument, such as a digital electronic balance or dissolved oxygen meter, can improve precision in measurements, allowing scientists to achieve more accurate results in lab work.

New ideas gleaned from science often bring a need for new technologies. These technologies, in turn, are developed by engineers and then utilized by scientists for further scientific investigations. The interconnectedness among scientific inquiry, engineering design, and technological development is reflected in the key roles each plays through the cycle of research and development.

The Impact of Science, Engineering, and Technology on Society

The interrelatedness of scientific knowledge, engineering solutions, and technological advances has had a profound and lasting effect on human society and the natural environment. For example, insights from scientific investigations have altered the way bridges are designed, crops are raised, surgery is performed, and machinery is produced.

Human society, in turn, influences science and engineering through its goals and expectations for technological developments. A range of economic, cultural, and political factors may drive decisions for improving or replacing technologies. Society also sets limits on the work of scientists and engineers, such as regulating the extraction of resources or in establishing acceptable levels of pollution from mining, farming, and industry.

A World of Engineering

Imagine a construction material that absorbs and destroys smog. Picture a robot that carries a patient and provides for other healthcare needs and comfort. Think about how solar panels built into roads could revolutionize highway travel. Engineers turn these and countless other ideas into reality. Those are just a few ways in which engineers use their science and math skills, and their creativity, to develop technologies for today and tomorrow.

Engineering and Chemistry

Chemistry plays a key role in many areas of engineering, from the development of pharmaceuticals and industrial chemicals to the design of materials used in everything from construction to clothing and cosmetics. A few areas of engineering that incorporate chemistry are described on the next page. These and other specialties in chemical engineering are discussed in more detail in Lesson 2.

Lesson 1: What Is Engineering? *continued*

When you think about chemical engineering, you may picture someone working at a lab bench filled with test tubes. For some types of chemical engineering, this image isn't incorrect. Many chemical engineers work in laboratories to design and test chemical formulations, from cosmetics to house paint to cleaning products. These engineers rely on a solid understanding of the most fundamental chemical reactions and processes.

Chemical engineers who work in food-processing industries contribute to the development of all kinds of food products. Chemical engineers also may work with bioengineers and agricultural engineers to design better crops and improve methods for pest control in agriculture.

Materials engineers use their knowledge of materials chemistry to design and test new fabrics, metals, plastics, concrete, and other materials. When designing structures such as bridges or buildings, civil engineers work closely with materials engineers to determine the best materials for the job.

A strong foundation in biochemistry is essential for engineers working in the various biotechnology industries. Some biotechnology engineers focus on developing pharmaceuticals, while others may work with cell or tissue cultures.

Petroleum engineers use their knowledge of chemistry and geology to improve methods for refining petroleum products. Some chemical engineers may use the same areas of knowledge to develop processes for cleaning toxic oil spills and related industrial accidents. Still others may work to develop biofuels and other fossil-fuel alternatives.

Questions

1. How might the interrelatedness of science, engineering, and technology drive the development of a new type of biofuel?

2. Briefly describe the impact that development of a new technique to mine copper might have on society, and how society might, in turn, have an impact on further development of similar technology.

Lesson 2: Engineering and Chemistry

Can you imagine modern life without aluminum? No soft drink cans, pots and pans, or foil wrapping. No car bumpers or fancy wheel rims, planes or ships or helicopters. No bikes or house siding or power lines that carry electricity to our homes and factories. Of course, some of these items—such as pots and pans—can be made of other metals. And some items are made of aluminum alloys, or mixtures of aluminum and other metals or nonmetal elements.

Pure aluminum has so many uses because it is a soft metal that bends easily into different shapes. But when aluminum is combined with other metals, it forms very strong alloys with unique physical properties. Who experiments with such combinations to determine the use of alloys? This is one of the jobs of a chemical engineer.

Engineering and the Metallurgy Industry

Although aluminum is the most common metal in Earth's crust, it is never found free in nature. Instead, it is combined with minerals as ores. Aluminum used to be very difficult to extract from its ore and, therefore, was among the most valuable of metals. In fact, when aluminum was chosen in 1884 as the cap and lightning rod to top the Washington Monument, it was more expensive than silver. Then, in 1886, American Charles Martin Hall and Frenchman Paul Héroult independently invented a process for separating aluminum from its ore by electrolysis. This process was so much easier that the price of aluminum quickly dropped, and chemical engineers developed thousands of uses for the metal and its alloys. The Hall-Héroult method is still used today.

Many chemical engineers specialize in metallurgical research. One of the unique alloys of aluminum that they have developed is shape-memory metal, a copper-aluminum-nickel alloy that "remembers" its original shape and springs back after it has been bent or twisted. Imagine twisting a pair of eyeglass frames into a knot. When the metal is warmed, the knot quickly unwinds.

Shape-memory metals have many medical applications. They are used as hooks to reconnect broken bones and as stents that expand clogged arteries and veins. Orthodontists often use shape-memory wires and dental braces to move teeth. A brace, also called an archwire, is molded to a person's mouth and inserted. As the archwire warms up in the mouth, it gradually reverts to its original shape, correcting poor teeth alignment and overcrowding. Shape-memory dental wires do not have to be adjusted and retightened as often as more traditional wires do, requiring fewer visits to the orthodontist.

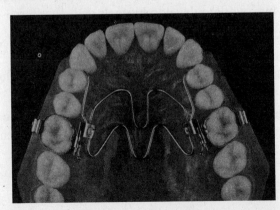

Engineering and the Chemical Industry

Many chemical engineers work in the chemical industry. This industry encompasses a wide range of products, from petroleum products and synthetic fibers and rubber to perfumes, medicines, and even foods. Once the need for a chemical product has been identified, engineers might experiment in a lab to develop a chemical process and then adapt the process for commercial production.

Chlorine gas is one of the most important chemicals in industry. It is commonly produced by electrolysis of sodium chloride solution and is used to kill harmful microorganisms in drinking water and swimming pools. It is also used to make hundreds of other products. Chemical engineers design manufacturing plants in which chemical products such as chlorine gas are made. The engineers develop the safe, efficient, and cost-effective technology for manufacturing. Because chlorine gas is highly toxic, engineers must be especially careful to design safe technology for manufacturing and handling chlorine.

Developing new polymers is of interest to many chemical engineers. A polymer is a macromolecule consisting of small molecules arranged in a simple repeating pattern. One new polymer has the potential to prevent explosions after a plane crash. Jet planes normally carry thousands of gallons of fuel. That fuel is highly flammable under crash conditions because it sprays into the air as a fine mist that often explodes on impact, making crash damage far worse. Chemical engineers have developed fuel additives that work by linking the sticky ends of polymer chains to form very long chains called mega-supramolecules. Because these extremely long chains have more than 50,000 carbon atoms in their structure, they are able to inhibit the formation of the explosive fuel mist. Post-crash explosions are reduced, and as a result, plane passengers have more time to escape the crash, and there is less damage to the plane.

Another new polymer has a very different function. Chemical engineers in France have recorded binary code on a synthetic polymer molecule. Like DNA, this molecule has the ability to hold enormous amounts of information. Instead of using DNA's four monomers, or building blocks, to encode information, this polymer uses three monomers. Two represent binary code numbers 0 and 1. The third monomer is inserted between the other two in order to make the writing and reading of the coded sequence easier. The engineering team that is working on the polymer hopes to develop molecular barcodes. The sequences on this polymer would provide labels that would be very difficult to copy or counterfeit, making it ideal for medicines or very expensive goods.

Many synthetic polymers are in everyday use, and all were developed by chemical engineers. Nylon fabrics, bulletproof vests, nonstick pans, and PVC pipes are examples. Even car and truck tires are made of synthetic polymers. Synthetic rubber was developed during World War II when the United States could no longer get natural rubber from Southeast Asia.

Engineering and the Food Industry

Cheesemakers in Switzerland have known for more than a century that Emmental Swiss cheese made during the summer has fewer holes than the same cheese made during the winter. They also noticed that the holes in the cheese, known as eyes, have gotten smaller over the past 15 years. They knew that the bacteria used in the cheese-making process release carbon dioxide, which forms bubbles that become the eyes. But they didn't know how or why the holes change from season to season and have become smaller. It took a team of Swiss food engineers to solve the mystery. The engineers used a CT scanner to

| Lesson 2: Engineering and Chemistry *continued*

follow the formation and ripening of Swiss cheese from milk over 130 days. Like all engineers, they combined science, technology, and ingenuity to solve the problem. Here is what they found.

In winter months, Swiss cows are fed hay. Before modern milking methods were developed, the cows' milk was collected in open buckets. Microscopically small particles of hay in the air fell into the buckets, and carbon dioxide bubbles formed around the particles, in much the same way that raindrops form around tiny dust particles in the air. As the cheese matured, the bubbles grew, resulting in larger eyes. In summer months, Swiss cows graze on grass in Alpine pastures. There are fewer hay particles in the barns to fall into the collected milk, resulting in fewer eyes. And in recent years, the eyes have gotten smaller because milk-processing plants have gotten cleaner. Cleaner air and closed milking machines have replaced open buckets, making it less likely that hay dust will fall into the milk.

Engineers in the food industry are also involved in designing food packaging. For example, they have recently designed a flip-top cap with a built-in measuring scoop for measuring out powdered food products such as ground coffee and protein powders. Previously, scoops put on top of the products inside their containers have worked their way to the bottom of the container during shipping. The buried scoops were hard to dig out of the powdered product and were less hygienic. The new built-in scoop ensures that it is always easily available.

Engineers have designed improved cereal containers too. Instead of the familiar cardboard box, some cereals come in a flexible pouch that closes with a side zipper. Engineers saw a need for resealable food packages for several reasons. Families have gotten smaller, and many households consist of only one or two people. Cereal has to stay fresh longer, and using resealable packages is a good way to accomplish that. Resealable, flexible pouches are lighter and more compact, so they reduce transportation costs for the manufacturer and take up less space on store and kitchen shelves. Engineers predict that many more products will soon be available in flexible, resealable pouches.

Engineering and the Pharmaceutical Industry

When you have a cold or bad headache, you might take a pain reliever. A lot of thought went into developing that medicine. Should the drug be in the form of a tablet, capsule, or liquid? Should it be buffered, or coated with an inert substance to prevent gastrointestinal upsets? Should substances be added to release the medicine slowly into the bloodstream over time? These are some of the questions a pharmaceutical engineer has to answer before a drug goes on the market.

Pharmaceutical engineers are involved in the development and manufacturing of drug products. They also work with scientists to discover and test new drugs. Like food engineers, pharmaceutical engineers may also be involved in designing the packaging and labeling of the end products. And they must make sure that the manufacturing process produces a safe and effective product that meets government standards.

Before a new drug can be formulated, its physical, chemical, and mechanical properties must be determined. For example, the active ingredient's pH, solubility, and particle size must be established. Only then can an engineer choose the inert ingredients to include in a tablet or capsule. Inert ingredients may be added to increase the active ingredient's stability in temperature and humidity variations, to "bulk up" the active ingredient, or to improve solubility. Compounds may also be added to improve the color or flavor of the pill. Inert materials are often added to improve the manufacturing process by decreasing the stickiness of the powdered active ingredient or by making the powder easier to handle on an assembly line. When these and other decisions have been made, a drug with consistent dosage, uniform appearance, acceptable taste, and adequate solubility is ready to be manufactured.

Finally, a new drug's packaging must be designed, depending on whether the drug is a solid, a liquid, or even a gas. Pills may be packaged in blister packs or bottles. Liquids and gases may be packaged in ready-filled syringes, aerosol cartridges, or vials. Decisions must even be made about the material of the container. Should it be glass, plastic, or metal? Tests have to be carried out to ensure that none of the ingredients interact with the container or that the drug doesn't absorb any of the container ingredients. Even the glue that holds the label in place must be tested to be sure it doesn't leach through the container into the drug. These are just some of the many tasks that pharmaceutical engineers must perform and decisions they must make before any medicine reaches the consumer.

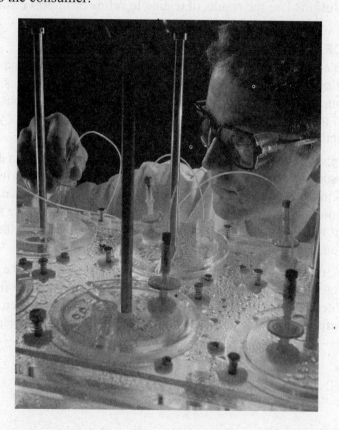

Questions

1. Suppose a cheese manufacturer wants to make a new type of cheese that tastes like Swiss cheese but has no holes. As a food engineer, what would you recommend that the manufacturer do?

2. What factors must a chemical engineer take into consideration when designing a plant to manufacture a toxic product such as chlorine gas?

Lesson 3: Engineering Design Process

Engineers typically follow a design process to develop the best solutions to problems. This lesson describes that process. You'll discover that the steps in the process can be used to design solutions to problems in your everyday life, such as preparing food or planning a trip, as well as larger problems, such as adding lights to your school's grounds. In the the activities that follow this lesson, you'll have the opportunity to apply the design process to several engineering problems.

Like scientific inquiry, engineering design is a process based on a set of practices that can be used in flexible ways. In general, you can think of the engineering design process as having three main phases:

- **Define and Delimit the Problem** Clearly state the problem, describe the characteristics of a successful solution, and identify any factors that limit the solution.

- **Design Solutions** Generate ideas for possible solutions; select and test the most promising design solution.

- **Optimize Solutions** Use the results of testing to refine or improve your solution.

DEFINE AND DELIMIT THE PROBLEM

When tackling an engineering challenge, the first step is to clearly define the problem to be solved. To define the problem, you need to identify the characteristics that a solution must have to be successful. You can think of these characteristics as your criteria for success. You also need to identify any factors that might limit or restrict your solution. These limiting factors are the constraints on your design solution.

To take a simple example, perhaps you need a recipe to make a main dish for dinner. Your criteria for success might be that the dish tastes delicious and that it is nutritious. Some constraints might be that the ingredients cost less than $10 and that the recipe can be made in one hour or less. If any of the friends you'll be serving have food allergies, another constraint would be that the recipe not include any ingredients that would cause an allergic reaction.

In many cases, it is not possible to find a solution that meets all of the criteria perfectly while staying within the constraints. For that reason, you may find it helpful to prioritize your criteria so that you can identify the best tradeoffs between criteria and constraints. A useful tool for this purpose is a Pugh chart like the one below.

CRITERIA	Maximum Value (1 to 5)	Solution A	Solution B	Solution C
Total Points				
CONSTRAINTS				
	Yes/No			
	Yes/No			
Which solution will you choose? Explain why.				

To use a Pugh chart to compare your solutions, follow these steps:
- List your criteria and constraints on the left side of the chart.
- List your possible solutions across the top.
- Prioritize your criteria by assigning a maximum value to each criterion, depending on how important it is.
- Rate each solution on how well it meets each criterion. If it meets the criterion perfectly, it gets the maximum value.
- Add up the points and indicate whether each solution meets all the constraints.

Design Solutions
After you have identified your criteria and constraints, you are ready to brainstorm possible solutions. Often you will also need to research the problem and explore the possibilities. You may need to study the details of the problem or different aspects of the systems that are involved. You should also review the solutions and processes that people have developed for similar problems. It can be easier and less risky to adapt an existing solution than to invent a new solution. For example, it is usually easier to use or adapt a recipe than to invent one. Existing solutions have already been through cycles of optimization, so many of the component problems and issues have already been resolved. The effects of the solutions, including unintended consequences, are already known. You might be able to choose the best of several possible solutions, you might adjust one solution to suit your problem, or you might combine parts of different solutions.

Lesson 3: Engineering Design Process *continued*

Generate or find multiple solutions or approaches. Use your knowledge and your research to imagine possible solutions. The first idea is not necessarily the best idea, so try to ensure that you have explored a wide range of possibilities. Sometimes an unworkable idea can lead to a better idea. After you have generated a good set of ideas, use the criteria and constraints to evaluate the most promising ones. The use of criteria and constraints can help you be objective, especially when evaluating your own ideas.

Once you have selected the most promising solution, you will need to test it to determine how well it actually performs. The results of your testing help you to learn more about your materials and the design of your system. Sometimes you may choose to test more than one solution and then combine the strong points of each design into a new and better design solution.

OPTIMIZE SOLUTIONS

You can use the results of your testing as feedback to refine and improve your solution. Some parts of your design may have worked well, while other parts were problematic. Focusing your attention on these problem areas will help you troubleshoot your design and come up with ideas for making it work better.

Testing, evaluating, and refining your solution should be an iterative process. That means you may repeat these steps in a series of design cycles to arrive at the best solution. These cycles of optimizing your solutions are often where the most important work takes place as you refine the details and make sure all the parts of your solution work together effectively.

REFLECT AND COMMUNICATE

As with any process or skill, you will become better at engineering design as you practice it and gain more experience. Thinking reflectively about your design process is one the best ways to improve. You may find it valuable to use a notebook to record notes about your design strategies and thinking as you work on developing a solution. Your notebook is also a place where you can make sketches and diagrams to explore your design ideas and to refine details of your design as you troubleshoot your solution.

The notes and sketches from your notebook can also be a valuable resources when it comes time to communicate your design solution to others. The ability to communicate effectively is a valuable skill for engineers and other designers, who often need to explain and promote their solutions to customers or clients. They may also publish details of their design process in technical journals, so that other engineers can build on their work.

Activity 1
Properties of Adobe

In this activity, you will design, construct, and test adobe bricks using a variety of materials.

BACKGROUND

The properties of a material determine its use. This is especially true in the construction industry. Researchers conduct extensive testing on materials to determine such properties as strength, compressibility, structural integrity, and resistance to thermal changes. Engineers analyze the testing results as they investigate possible uses for the materials.

One of the earliest construction materials ever used is adobe. This material is a mixture of soil (mostly clay but also sand and silt), water, and fibrous organic materials such as straw. The fibrous material is a binding agent that holds the material together and gives it strength, similar to what rebar does in concrete. An adobe mixture can be pressed into molds to form bricks of uniform shape and size. The mortar that holds these bricks together usually has a composition that is similar to the brick, minus the fibrous material.

Adobe often is used in areas where daytime temperatures are high and evening temperatures are low. Because of adobe's thermal properties, the bricks absorb heat during the warm day and then slowly release it during the cool evening. These actions help moderate the temperature inside the adobe structure throughout the day and night.

Components of the adobe material must be mixed carefully to maintain consistent and quality bricks. Too much of one component or too little of another could compromise the strength and thermal properties of the brick. Studies have shown that the proportions of soil materials should be no more than one-third clay, no less than one-half sand, and no more than one-third silt to produce optimal structural and thermal properties.

Careful consideration also must be given to the way in which the brick dries. If it dries too quickly, it could crack; if it dries too slowly, it may never set enough to be removed from the mold. The mixture should dry at a reasonable pace so that the bricks can be removed and the molds quickly reused. Drying begins in the mold. Then the brick is removed from the mold and is usually placed in the shade so it can finish drying slowly without cracking. Full drying time depends on the particular mixture and on the humidity and temperature of the region.

Adobe has a lot going for it as a construction material. It is strong and durable, and it offers thermal properties that are useful in climates with extreme temperature changes from day to night. It can be made from local materials and is inexpensive. It is relatively low-tech, requiring minimal tools. All of these qualities make adobe a good material choice in many underdeveloped countries, especially in small villages and other remote areas.

Activity 1: Properties of Adobe *continued*

But adobe isn't perfect. Besides problems with cracking, if the mix is too wet and the bricks do not set properly, erosion from rain can weaken them. The success of adobe depends on using the right proportions of materials under the right conditions. That's the challenge.

Materials

Use materials that your teacher provides or those of your choice.

SAFETY

- Wear safety goggles and an apron at all times.
- Handle sharp objects such as trowels and nails carefully.

DESIGN CHALLENGE

Objective: Design, construct, and test adobe bricks for properties associated with resistance to breaking that would make the brick a useful material for construction.

By experimenting with the type and quantity of materials, you can collect data that will allow engineers to help people build better adobe structures. Your team's challenge is to design, construct, and test a series of adobe bricks using a variety of recipes.

DEFINE AND DELIMIT THE PROBLEM

Research the conditions required for designing and constructing adobe bricks. Look for the proportions of soil, water, and organic material and consider how these components should be mixed to ensure the best brick. Research the time and conditions needed for your bricks to dry, including when to remove them from the molds and when to test them. Consider and follow all safety practices as you work.

Consider other materials that could be added to increase the strength of your bricks. Focus on materials that would be available in a particular region where adobe bricks would be widely used. Then list the criteria and constraints of your design solution.

Activity 1: Properties of Adobe *continued*

Criteria and Constraints

_____

_____

_____

_____

_____

_____

_____

_____

_____

_____

DESIGN SOLUTIONS

Determine how many adobe recipes you will test and what those recipes will be. You will need to think about the brick size. Then you will have to design and build a mold that will be used to cast the bricks. You might choose three to six recipes to test, or you might choose two or three recipes but for bricks of two different shapes or sizes. You might want to use small bricks to minimize drying time and for ease of testing. A convenient size is about 15 cm by 8 cm (about the size of a smartphone) with a thickness of 3 to 5 cm. All bricks must have the same dimensions for experimental results to be valid. Also consider how to remove each brick from the mold without damaging the brick.

How will you test the strength of your bricks, and will this process be repeatable for all bricks tested? Determine how your testing process will allow you to collect quantitative data and how you will display the data.

One common form of testing involves dropping the bricks from increasing heights until the bricks crack or break into fragments. How will you ensure that the bricks will be dropped in the same way and land at the same angle? What kind of surface will they land on?

When you have chosen the design of the bricks and the mold, sketch them in the spaces on the next page. Verify your brick making and testing procedures with your teacher. Then, build your molds and make your bricks.

Name _____ Class _____ Date _____

Activity 1: Properties of Adobe *continued*

Design Sketch — Brick

Design Sketch — Mold

OPTIMIZE YOUR SOLUTION

Before testing your bricks, be sure to establish criteria for what constitutes a failed brick. Determine how each brick will be dropped to ensure consistency in how each brick lands. Remember, you can modify a design or procedure at any time if problems arise during construction and testing, but be sure to retest any modifications you make.

Record your test results on the next page. In the Notes section, record any issues related to the experimental design. Also note what changes you might make to improve the success of the adobe bricks or to trade off less important features for those that are more important. Finally, explain how your design addresses the problem you are trying to solve.

Name _____ Class _____ Date _____

Test Results

Brick	Size	Mixture Recipe	Fail Height
1			
2			
3			
4			
5			
6			

Notes on Test

_____

_____

_____

_____

_____

_____

_____

_____

For accuracy, you may wish to re-create each brick set and retest the new bricks to ensure that the results are repeatable. Create one or more graphs in the space below to illustrate your findings. Use another sheet of paper if necessary.

Graphs

Activity 1: Properties of Adobe *continued*

Answer the following questions about your adobe bricks and tests.

1. Which of the brick recipes you tested best met the criteria for your design solution? Explain why.

_____

_____

_____

_____

_____

2. What challenges did you encounter in testing your bricks? How might you modify your testing procedure if you repeated the experiment?

_____

_____

_____

_____

_____

_____

EXTENSION

Design an experiment that uses your bricks in a model wall and test the effect of compression on this model. Consider how you could design, build, and test a series of larger walls of your most effective adobe recipe to support a more massive roof on a dwelling. Build the model wall and perform your tests, with teacher approval and using all safety measures. Communicate your results through an oral presentation or written report. Consider using video of the tests in your presentation.

Activity 2
Design a Treatment to Clear a Blood Clot

In this activity, you will design, test, and revise a treatment to clear a blockage from a model blood clot.

BACKGROUND

Blood is a complex fluid composed of plasma, blood cells, platelets, and a variety of dissolved biomolecules. It flows through our circulatory system, pushed by the constant beating of the heart. Blood is essential for life. Every cell in the body depends on blood for the delivery of nutrients and the removal of waste. If blood is lost through even the tiniest cut, the body has a natural defense to stop the bleeding: a blood clot forms.

Clot formation, or coagulation, is an important function of the body. However, abnormalities in the process can lead to severe complications. If there is excessive clotting and a blood clot forms in a blood vessel, it could lead to a heart attack or stroke. Some biomedical engineers work to develop solutions to prevent blood clots from forming or to remove ones that already exist. Some treatments involve surgical removal of the clot, while others utilize chemicals to reduce the size of the clot and allow blood to resume a normal flow.

In this activity, you will develop a chemical treatment for the removal of a model blood clot. The model is a piece of white polymer that clogs a length of clear, flexible tubing. The polymer clog is produced by mixing borax, water, and polyvinyl acetate from white glue.

This combination of reactants has two results. One, the borax and water form the following borate-boric acid buffer system in which the products and reactants are in chemical equilibrium:

$$B(OH)_3 + 2H_2O \rightleftharpoons B(OH)_4^- + H_3O^+$$

Two, the polyvinyl acetate chemically changes, and the $B(OH)_4^-$ causes the polymer chains to cross-link, trapping water and resulting in the rubbery white polymer clog. Using what you know about how the clog was formed, you will design a chemical treatment to degrade the clog and restore flow in the tube.

Activity 2: Design a Treatment to Clear a Blood Clot *continued*

SAFETY

- Wear safety goggles, an apron, and gloves at all times.
- Handle glassware and all chemicals safely. Do not pour water into strong acids or strong bases, as they may produce heat and splatter.
- If a chemical spills on the floor, clean it up as instructed by your teacher.
- Dispose of all chemicals properly, as directed by your teacher.

Materials

- paper cups
- wooden stirrers
- marker for labeling cups
- white glue
- 4% borax solution
- water
- graduated cylinder (50 mL)
- 1 M HCl
- 1 M NaOH
- NaCl solution
- glucose solution
- liquid detergent

DESIGN CHALLENGE

Objective: Design, test, and revise a treatment to remove a polymer clog from a length of clear, flexible tubing, which is a model for a blood clot in a blood vessel.

The first step is to recreate the white polymer clog to understand what exactly you have to remove. You will do that in Part 1 by synthesizing four different samples of the white polymer, comparing them to the given model, and selecting the sample that best matches the model, based on your observations. Then in Part 2 you will design and test your treatment on this sample, and, based on those results, in Part 3, you will test your treatment on the model blood clot. After a round of testing, you will try to improve the performance of your treatment system.

Activity 2: Design a Treatment to Clear a Blood Clot *continued*

PART 1

The first step is to discover the nature of the model "blood clot" (the white polymer clog) so that you can design an effective process for its removal. You will make four polyvinyl acetate polymers using the proportions in the table below.

1. Label the cups as polymers 1, 2, 3, and 4.

2. Measure 15 mL of water in the graduated cylinder and pour it into cup 1. Mark the level of water in the cup and pour out the water. Mark the same 15 mL level on the other cups.

3. Fill each cup up to the 15 mL line with white glue. (Do not use the graduated cylinder to measure the glue.)

4. For each polymer, add the amounts of borax solution and water indicated in the table.

5. Stir well until each polymer is formed. Knead for a minute or two. Record your observations in the table.

Polymer	Volume (mL)			Observations
	Glue	**Water**	**Borax**	
1	15	20	5	
2	15	30	10	
3	15	40	5	
4	15	40	20	

Based on your observations, which polymer is the best match for the model blood clot that your teacher provided? Explain your reasoning.

_____

_____

_____

| Activity 2: Design a Treatment to Clear a Blood Clot *continued*

PART 2

Next you will use the polymer you selected to predict how well each of the following liquids would break down the model blood clot:

- 1 M HCl
- 1 M NaOH
- NaCl solution
- glucose solution
- liquid detergent

Sketch and describe the procedure you will use to test the liquids. Be sure to include the materials you will use and how you will use them.

Design Sketch

After your teacher approves your procedure, carry out the experiment and record your results below. Which of the liquids would you recommend for the treatment of the model blood clot?

_____

_____

_____

_____

_____

_____

| Activity 2: Design a Treatment to Clear a Blood Clot *continued*

DEFINE AND DELIMIT THE PROBLEM

For your chemical treatment of the clot, consider how much of the blockage should be removed. Should the blockage be loosened or completely broken down? Think about how you will administer the treatment, the quantity you will use, and how quickly the treatment should work. Though your challenge utilizes a *model* blood clot, keep in mind the practical issues of treating actual blood clots. Consider also the time, materials, and cost for your treatment. Then write a list of the criteria and constraints for your design.

PART 3: OPTIMIZE YOUR SOLUTION

Now it's time to test the treatment. Your teacher will designate a place and time for you to test your treatment on the actual model blood clot. Again, record thorough observations of your treatment.

In the Notes section, record where and how any failures occurred. Based on your notes and observations, describe what changes you might make to improve the treatment to trade off less important features for those that are more important. Decide on which changes you want to make, implement those changes, and then retest your modified treatment on another model blood clot. Be sure to record all data associated with the modification. Also, explain how your design addresses the problem you are trying to solve. Describe how you are changing the conditions of the chemical equilibrium to arrive at the desired result.

Test Results – Part 3: Chemical Treatment of Model Blood Clot

	Observations
Test on Model Blood Clot	

Activity 2: Design a Treatment to Clear a Blood Clot continued

Notes on Test

_____

_____

_____

_____

_____

_____

_____

_____

_____

_____

_____

_____

_____

_____

_____

_____

_____

_____

_____

_____

_____

_____

_____

_____

_____

Activity 2: Design a Treatment to Clear a Blood Clot *continued*

Answer the following questions about your treatment.

1. Compare the original version of your treatment with the version after your modifications. Explain why you chose to modify your treatment.

_____

_____

_____

_____

_____

2. Which criteria did you find most difficult to meet?

_____

_____

_____

_____

_____

3. Why was it important to re-create the model blood clot at the beginning of the design process? How is this step similar to what biomedical engineers do in order to develop treatments?

_____

_____

_____

_____

_____

_____

Activity 2: Design a Treatment to Clear a Blood Clot *continued*

EXTENSION

Consider again the chemical equilibrium that resulted in the formation of the model blood clot. What other treatments could you devise for clearing the clot? In what other ways could you affect the equilibrium to reach the desired result? Design another treatment scheme, including a list of the materials you would need and a detailed procedure. With teacher approval, carry out your treatment on another model blood clot. Communicate your results to the class.

Activity 3
Design an Improved Detergent

In this activity, you will test the effectiveness of different detergents and use the results to design a detergent with optimal ingredients for removing stains.

BACKGROUND

Chances are, you or your family has used detergent recently, probably for washing dishes or clothes. Detergents, like hand soaps, break up and remove grease, soil, and other materials that attach to a surface and make it dirty.

The most important ingredients in detergents are chemicals known as surface-active agents, or surfactants. Surfactants reduce the surface tension of water, allowing the water to spread and soak surfaces quickly and completely. Surfactant molecules are long chains with a hydrophobic (water-fearing) end and a hydrophilic (water-loving) end. The hydrophobic end of the molecule is attracted to grease and dirt, which allows the soapy solution to pick up and wash away these particles.

Other additives in detergents serve specific purposes. For example, some laundry detergent additives brighten colors of clothing and add pleasant scents. Additives also help target specific types of stains such as those from proteins, fatty molecules, and starchy molecules. These additives are in the form of enzymes that target and break up the specific type of molecules. Some additives can be combined in one detergent to target a variety of stains. However, combining too many additives may have drawbacks because some additives might affect the performance of others and thus cannot be used together for maximum effectiveness. These considerations must be taken into account when determining the best formulation for a detergent.

Materials

Use materials that your teacher provides or those of your choice.

SAFETY

• Wear safety goggles, gloves, and an apron at all times.

• Handle all chemicals carefully.

DESIGN CHALLENGE

Objective: Design an optimal formulation for a detergent to remove stains from clothing based on tests of commercially available laundry detergents.

You will design and perform an experiment to determine which of several detergents works best to clean a particular stain. You will then research key ingredients in the detergents to determine which are important in removing the stain and use this information, along with your test results, to design a "new and improved" detergent.

| Activity 3: Design an Improved Detergent *continued* |

DEFINE AND DELIMIT THE PROBLEM

Research how detergents are made and how they work to remove stains. Then consider the criteria and constraints for your detergent test as well as for the new detergent you will design. The main criterion for the test will relate to how well the detergent cleans. You might consider other criteria that would be important to consumers, such as the form of the product (such as liquid, granular, small packets). What other criteria do you want your detergent to have?

When thinking about constraints, consider safety to the environment. For example, phosphates improve the performance of detergents, but these chemicals also act as fertilizers that cause algal blooms in streams and ponds. Consider also the cost of ingredients and manufacturing. Then list the criteria and constraints of your project.

Criteria and Constraints

_____

_____

_____

_____

_____

_____

_____

DESIGN SOLUTIONS

Brainstorm with your team to determine the best way to design your experiment to test different detergents. How many detergents will you test? Choose detergents that best meet the criteria and constraints you set. Try to include at least one organic detergent and one detergent that can be used in cold water.

Establish independent and dependent variables for your experiment. What kind of stain will you use? What kind of fabric will you stain? How will you ensure that the same amount and density of staining substance is present on each fabric sample? Consider all aspects of the test. For instance, will you agitate (swirl) the fabric in the detergent solution to model the action in a washing machine? If so, how?

In the space below, outline the procedure for your experiment. Be sure the procedure is repeatable so that you can compare results. Provide a sketch of the setup or key steps. With your teacher's approval, conduct your experiment and record your results in the data table below. Remember, you can modify a procedure at any time if problems arise during testing, but be sure to retest any modifications you make. In the Notes section, record where and how any issues related to the experimental design occurred.

Activity 3: Design an Improved Detergent *continued*

Procedure and Sketch for Testing Detergents

Test Results

Detergent	Formulation (Key Ingredients)	Stain	Observations
1			
2			
3			
4			
5			

Activity 3: Design an Improved Detergent *continued*

Notes on Test

_____

_____

_____

_____

_____

_____

_____

_____

OPTIMIZE YOUR SOLUTION

Analyze your test results to determine which key ingredients were most important to removing the stain. Use this information, along with other properties that best meet your criteria, to design a "new and improved" detergent. For example, your best test results may have been from a detergent that includes a specific enzyme. Another detergent might have a certain fragrance or softening agent that is among your criteria. Consider such factors as you work with your team to design a better detergent. You may need to do further research on the enzymes or other additives you are considering to make sure they would perform as expected.

Below, record the ingredients that you think would result in an improved detergent. Explain how the ingredients would meet your criteria and address the problem you are trying to solve.

Design of Improved Detergent

_____

_____

_____

_____

_____

_____

| Activity 3: Design an Improved Detergent *continued*

Answer the following questions about your detergent experiment.

1. How did you ensure that the tests were accurate and repeatable?

   _____

   _____

   _____

   _____

   _____

   _____

2. What are some sources of error that may have affected your test results?

   _____

   _____

   _____

   _____

   _____

   _____

EXTENSION

Design a test as part of a challenge to develop a product that could be used to clean up an oil spill that washes to shore. You will need to research the properties of products that are used for such purposes. Your test might focus on dishwashing detergents rather than laundry detergents. First, determine which existing product best meets the criteria for a safe and effective cleaner. Then try to design an improved product to solve the problem of cleaning up oil that comes in contact with the living and nonliving parts of a shoreline.

Activity 4
Design a Radiant Floor Heating System

In this activity, you will use specific heat data to design, build, and test a model of a radiant heating system for a home.

BACKGROUND

Specific heat is the amount of energy needed to raise the temperature of 1 g of a substance by 1°C or 1 K. A metal with a higher specific heat is better able to absorb and then release that heat than is a metal with a lower specific heat. This property of metals and other materials is important in the construction industry. Solar collectors, electric baseboard heaters, radiant floor heating, and heat exchange systems all take advantage of the ability of metals to absorb and release heat.

Consider one of these applications—a radiant floor heating system. Such a system usually consists of an array of hot-water-carrying tubes arranged in a pattern under the subflooring. The water's heat warms the floor and, ultimately, the space above it. When designing a radiant floor heating system, engineers must decide on the materials used to dissipate and reflect the heat within the system. If a material will not absorb a large quantity of heat, or takes too long to absorb it, the system will not be very effective. This is where engineers use knowledge about the specific heat of metals and other materials to design a heating system that is efficient and effective.

Materials

Use materials that your teacher provides or those of your choice.

SAFETY

- Wear safety goggles and an apron at all times.
- Handle hot objects carefully, using tongs when needed.
- Handle sharp objects carefully. Cutting metal sheets into pieces can result in sharp edges.

DESIGN CHALLENGE

Objective: Design, construct, and test a small-scale radiant floor heating system based on the heat absorption capacities of different materials.

Different metals absorb and release heat at different rates. Through research, you can collect information to determine the best metals and other materials to use for a radiant floor heating system. Your team's challenge is to design, construct, and test a small model of such a system.

Activity 4: Design a Radiant Floor Heating System *continued*

DEFINE AND DELIMIT THE PROBLEM

Research the basic design of a radiant floor heating system. Consider criteria and constraints for the model system that you will design and build. The main criterion is that the system must use hot water to heat a room in a relatively short period of time. (Keep in mind that your model "room" might be only the size of a shoebox or shirt box.) Consider also the specific heat capacities of various metals and other materials and how these values relate to the material's ability to transmit heat quickly. Consider constraints of cost. For example, a certain metal may have a specific heat that makes it ideal for transmitting heat quickly but is too costly for this model as well as for a full-scale home system. Engineers often need to decide how to achieve a balance between cost and efficiency when determining the solution to a problem. Think about safety as well. Then list the criteria and constraints of your heating system.

Criteria and Constraints

_____

_____

_____

_____

_____

_____

_____

_____

_____

_____

DESIGN SOLUTIONS

As you research radiant floor heating systems, consider design options. Brainstorm with your team. You might combine features of different designs and/or make adjustments to those found in an existing system. Regardless of other design features, your basic model system should include a tubing array and a method for delivering a steady flow of hot water through the array. An effective way to do this is to connect one end of the tubing to a source of hot water, such as a tap, and place the other end at a drain or in a sink or large collection container. If a tap is not available, consider attaching the tubing to a funnel into which you can pour hot water. Ensure that hot water is available to flow through the system long enough to take effective temperature measurements.

Activity 4: Design a Radiant Floor Heating System *continued*

Consider the type of flooring you will use, both the subfloor beneath the tube array and the main floor above it. Think about the specific heat and thermal conductivity of the flooring material. Carpet, for example, will offer a greater resistance to heat transfer than will tile or wood.

During your research, you may find systems that use metal arrangements to direct the heat from the tubing upward, delivering it more effectively to the floor. Incorporate such arrangements into your design. Consider what metals to use, how to arrange them, and where to place them.

When you have chosen your design, sketch it in the space below. Decide on the best procedures for building and testing your radiant floor heating system model. Verify your procedure with your teacher. Then, build your model.

Design Sketch

OPTIMIZE YOUR SOLUTION

Now it's time to test the effectiveness of your system. What must happen to conclude that the system is effective? For example, will a small increase in surface temperature indicate success? Be sure to establish your criteria for a successful test before you conduct it. Remember, you can modify a design or procedure at any time if problems arise during construction and testing, but be sure to retest any modifications you make.

Record your test results below. (The chart allows for testing different systems if you wish to make and test modifications.) In the Notes section, record where and how any issues related to the experimental design occurred. Also note what additional changes you might make to improve the success of the system or to trade off less important features for those that are more important. Finally, explain how your design addresses the problem you are trying to solve.

| Activity 4: Design a Radiant Floor Heating System *continued*

Test Results

System	Area to be Heated	Description of System	Materials Used	Surface Temperature Change
1				
2				
3				
4				
5				
6				

Notes on Test

_____

_____

_____

_____

_____

_____

_____

Answer the following questions about your model system and its test.

1. Which constraints regarding the metal arrangements and their location in the system were most problematic? How did you solve these problems?

_____

_____

_____

_____

_____

_____

2. Which constraints regarding the testing of the system were most problematic? How did you solve these problems?

_____

_____

_____

_____

_____

_____

EXTENSION

Design a model system that could be used to cool a room rather than heat it. Consider what parts of your existing system you could use. Consider also the location of the cooling system. A radiant heating system should be installed in the floor, but is this the best location for a cooling system? What part or parts of your existing system must change, and how? Design, build, and test your new system, with teacher approval. Communicate your results by writing a report or giving an oral presentation to the class.

Activity 5
Design a Better Battery

In this activity, you will construct a copper-zinc wet cell battery that has a reliable voltage and then improve the design of your battery to increase storage capacity and ability to recharge.

BACKGROUND

Batteries are convenient sources of electrical energy. Although they are relatively simple devices, their design takes into account many factors, including the materials they are made of and the arrangement of their components. Considerations such as total voltage, storage capacity, weight, and durability determine what materials to use. Researchers conduct tests on the electrochemistry of materials and evaluate the advantages or disadvantages for the construction of batteries for specific purposes. Engineers optimize the combination of materials for cost, longevity, and other factors depending on the battery's intended use.

Batteries are constructed from materials that release electrical energy through chemical reactions. Often, these reactions can be reversed by using electricity to push the chemical reaction in the opposite direction. This requires a recharge voltage that is slightly higher than the cell voltage.

One type of battery uses wet cells. Such cells are made of an electrolyte and electrodes. The electrodes sometimes do not participate in the chemical reaction but act as a location to collect and move electrons. When a circuit is connected across the electrodes, a chemical reaction in the electrolyte transfers electrons as one electrode gains these electrons and the other electrode loses them. A voltage occurs across the electrodes, and the cell can be used to store electrical energy. The voltage depends on many factors, including the type of electrolyte. The amount of the reactants and products in each cell helps determine the storage capacity of the battery. Using several cells combined in series increases the voltage.

One type of electrolytic cell uses a lead oxide–sulphuric acid chemical reaction: the lead-acid battery. This battery is fairly inexpensive to produce but uses a strong, concentrated acid and potentially toxic materials. It is also very heavy, and spills can be difficult to manage. Other battery types include nickel-iron, lithium ion, and copper-zinc. Current battery development is focused on increasing the total storage capacity, decreasing production costs, and using batteries to store energy produced from alternate sources, such as solar.

Materials

Use materials that your teacher provides or those of your choice.

SAFETY

- Wear safety goggles and an apron at all times.

- Handle copper sulfate solution carefully, as it may stain clothing.

Activity 5: Design a Better Battery *continued*

DESIGN CHALLENGE

Objective: Design, build, test, and modify a rechargeable battery to maximize its electrical storage capacity, as measured by keeping a light bulb lit as long as possible, using 1.0 M solutions.

To meet this challenge, your team will be combining knowledge of simple circuits and wet cell chemistry. You will first consider criteria for making a copper-zinc wet cell. You will consider the variables of capacity and ability to recharge and some factors of those variables, such as volume of the cell and design of the electrodes. After you construct your wet cell, your team will seek to improve its performance.

DEFINE AND DELIMIT THE PROBLEM

Research the setup up of a wet cell battery, including the electrolyte solutions to use and the construction of the solid components, such as a salt bridge and electrodes. Use a simple circuit with a flashlight bulb to test your battery. Consider criteria and constraints. Your main criterion is that your design must optimize the capacity of a rechargeable copper-zinc wet cell. Consider how the shape and surface area of the electrode affects the operation of the battery. Think about cost, safety, and time constraints. Then list the criteria and constraints of your battery project.

Criteria and Constraints

_____

_____

_____

_____

_____

_____

_____

DESIGN SOLUTIONS

Decide how you will design and construct a copper-zinc wet cell. You might use the design of similar wet cells you have made in class previously, or you might research other designs. This wet cell will be your control, which you will compare with other wet cells you design in an attempt to improve performance. In the space on the next page, sketch the design of your control. Then build your control wet cell.

Activity 5: Design a Better Battery *continued*

Design Sketch – Control Wet Cell

[ ]

Use the data table on the next page to record the electrode design, voltage, and capacity of your control. You may need to make minor adjustments to the control until it works satisfactorily. Revise your sketch of the control to include any adjustments you make.

OPTIMIZE YOUR SOLUTION

To improve your battery, research how different electrode designs affect the operation of a wet cell, including recharging. Based on your research, brainstorm with your team ways to modify the electrodes. Incorporate your ideas as you design a comparison wet cell that you could test against the control. Be sure to change only one variable. For example, you might change the size, shape, configuration, or number of electrodes.

Sketch the comparison wet cell in the space on the next page. You might sketch only the part of the setup that you have changed, such as the electrodes. Show your design to your teacher. Then, with your teacher's permission, build your new wet cell and test its performance. Record the results in the data table.

If your teacher permits, continue to modify and test your wet cell to optimize its design, based on the results of your previous designs. Remember to change only one variable at a time. Adjust the variable until the results no longer show improvement in capacity or voltage, and then move on to another variable. As you work iteratively, analyze your sketches and results to look for patterns that improve capacity.

In the Notes section, record any issues that occurred during the iterative process. Explain how well your optimal design meets the criteria you set. Also note what changes you might make to improve the performance of your wet cell beyond the constraints you set.

Activity 5: Design a Better Battery *continued*

Design Sketches – Comparison Wet Cells

Test Results

Trial	Electrode design	Voltage (V)	Capacity (min)
Control			
1			
2			
3			
4			
5			
6			

Activity 5: Design a Better Battery *continued*

Notes

_____

_____

_____

_____

_____

_____

_____

_____

Create a graph to illustrate your findings in the space below. Graph each wet-cell capacity compared to the control.

Graph

Activity 5: Design a Better Battery *continued*

Answer the following questions about your wet cells and their tests.

1. What was the purpose of the control wet cell?

   _____

   _____

   _____

2. Which design feature of the wet cell was most difficult to work with? How did this difficulty affect the results?

   _____

   _____

   _____

   _____

EXTENSION

After optimizing the capacity of your wet cell design, consider the most cost-effective way to store 10 minutes of lighting, using the flashlight bulb. Consider connecting the cells in series or parallel as well as the volumes or concentrations. Communicate your results by writing a report or giving an oral presentation to the class. Include a demonstration of the wet cells in operation.